teach me about

Illness

Copyright © Joy Berry, 2022
Originally Published, 1986

All rights are reserved.

No part of this book can be duplicated or used without the prior written permission of the copyright owner, except for the use of brief quotations from the book.

For inquiries or permission requests contact the publisher.

Published by Joy Berry Enterprises
www.joyberryenterprises.com

teach me about

By JOY BERRY

Illustrated by Bartholomew

I like myself.

I do not want to get sick.

I want to stay well.

I eat good food.

It is good for me.

Good food helps me stay well.

I get sick when I get too cold.

I wear warm clothes
when it is cold.

Warm clothes help me stay well.

I play outside whenever I can.

It is good for me.

Fresh air and sunshine

help me stay well.

I exercise my body.

It is good for me.

Exercise helps me stay well.

I get sick when I get too tired.

I rest when I am tired.

Rest helps me stay well.

I go to the doctor's office for checkups.

Sometimes I get a shot.

The shot keeps me from getting sick.

Shots help me stay well.

Sometimes I get sick.

I do not like being sick.

I do things to get well.

Sometimes I go to the doctor

when I am sick.

I find out what is wrong with me.

The doctor tells me

what to do to get well.

Sometimes I get a shot.

The shot helps me to get well.

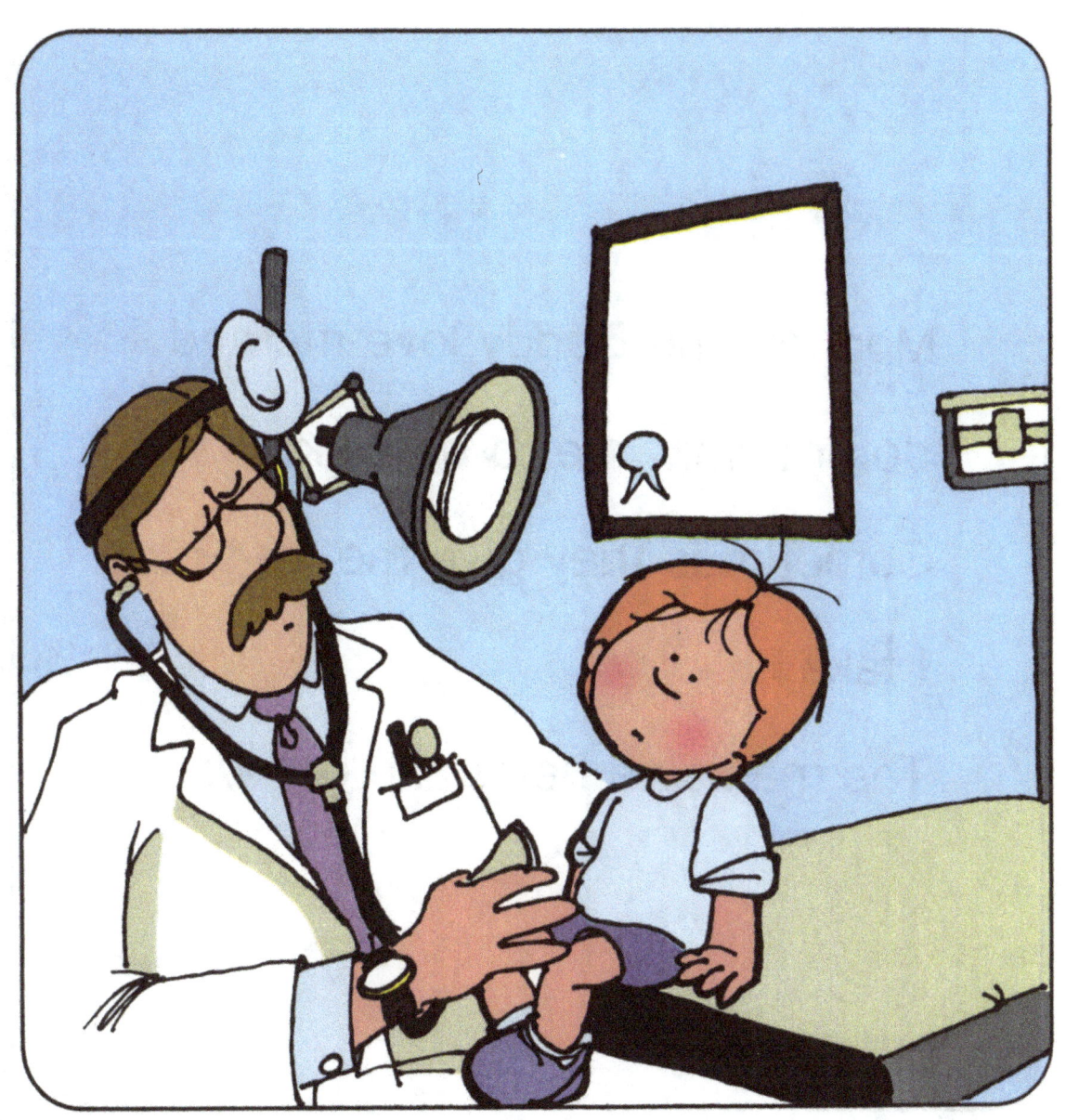

Mommy and Daddy love me and do not want me to be sick.

Sometimes they give me medicine.

I take it.

The medicine helps me get well.

I drink lots of water and juice when I am sick.

The water and juice help me to get well.

I rest when I am sick.

Resting helps me to get well.

Sometimes I get hurt.

Mommy and Daddy

help fix the hurt.

They clean it.

They put medicine on it.

Sometimes they put

a bandage on it.

I am careful with the hurt.

I want it to get well.

I like myself.

I want to stay well.

I take care of myself

so that I won't get sick.

I like being healthy.

helpful hints for parents about illness

Dear Parents:
The purpose of this book is—
    to show children what they can do to avoid illness, and
    to teach sick children what they can do to help themselves get well.
You can best implement the purpose of this book by—
    reading it to your child, and
    reading the following *Helpful Hints* and using them whenever applicable.

AVOIDING ILLNESS

Find a caring, competent physician. Take your child to him/her for regular checkups.

Check with your doctor concerning the following recommended tests and immunizations:

2 months)	
4 months)	D.P.T. shots (pertussis, tetanus, and
6 months)	oral polio)
1 year	Tuberculin test
15 months	Measles, mumps, and rubella shots
18 months	D.P.T. plus polio booster
5 years	D.P.T. plus polio booster
10 years	D.P.T. plus polio booster

Give your child the recommended doses of vitamins and minerals every day. Be sure to include vitamin C.

PREPARING FOR ILLNESS

Be ready to deal with any childhood illness by doing the following:

Emergency Numbers

Post these emergency numbers on or near your telephone:
- the doctor
- the fire station
- the police station
- the ambulance and/or paramedics
- the hospital
- the poison control center

Be sure you have these medicines, salves, and ointments on hand. Consult your physician for specific brand names, and read the directions carefully before administering them.

Medicines

- baby aspirin or an aspirin substitute (for fever and pain)
- a decongestant (for congestion)
- cough syrup (for coughs)
- glycerin suppositories (for constipation)
- syrup of ipecac (to induce vomiting)
- vitamin C for colds

Salves and Ointments
- aloe vera (for burns)
- antibiotic salve (for cuts and scrapes)
- vitamin E oil (to minimize scarring)
- anti-itch cream (for rashes and bites)
- hydrogen peroxide (for cleaning affected areas)
- alcohol (for sterilizing affected areas)
- sunscreen
- insect repellent
- diaper rash ointment

Miscellaneous Medical Supplies
Be sure you have these medical supplies on hand:
- a thermometer
- a humidifier
- cold compresses
- tweezers
- gauze
- an assortment of bandages

HANDLING COMMON HEALTH PROBLEMS

Here are some suggested procedures for dealing with common health problems.

Colds
- Give your child vitamin C (consult your physician for exact dosage).
- Elevate your child's head by raising the top end of the bed or mattress.
- Increase the humidity in the bedroom with a cold-mist humidifier.

Constipation
- Have your child drink fruit juice as it is a natural laxative.
- Use a glycerin suppository when all else fails. Consult your physician first.

Cuts
- Apply pressure to stop the bleeding of a cut.
- Clean the cut with hydrogen peroxide.
- Apply vitamin E oil.
- Bandage the cut if necessary.

Dehydration
- Put your child into a tub of running water and make a game of drinking from your hands or the faucet.
- Give your child diluted fruit juice, flavored drinks, crushed ice, or Popsicles.

Diaper Rash
- Add one-half cup baking soda to the wash cycle and one cup white distilled vinegar to the final rinse cycle when washing diapers.
- Change the diapers often.
- Wash the affected area with mild soap and clean water (avoid using prepackaged wipes). If the skin is very red, splash it with warm water.
- Dry the skin with a nonasbestos hair dryer. Put the dryer on the coolest setting. Test the warmth of your own skin and hold the dryer at least six inches from the baby's skin.
- Apply moisture-repellent ointment with vitamins A and D added.
- Discontinue giving fruit juice. (The acidity in the fruit juice may be causing the rash.)
- Offer water between meals to dilute the urine.
- Let your child go diaperless whenever possible. (The fresh air can help heal the rash.)

Heat Rash
- Apply cornstarch to the affected areas.
- Dress your child in fewer clothes.
- Put your child in cooler surroundings.

Insect Bites
- Clean the bitten area with vinegar.
- Apply a baking soda and water paste, calamine lotion, or an anti-itch cream.

Splinters
- Locate a hidden splinter by dabbing iodine on the general area. (The splinter will darken and will be easier to find.)
- Soak the affected area in warm water and/or vegetable oil.
- Numb the area with an ice cube.
- Remove the splinter with tweezers.

Sunburn
- Avoid sunburns by keeping your child in the shade, using a sunscreen lotion, and dressing him/her in a brimmed hat and high-necked shirt.
- Consult your physician if your child has a severe sunburn.
- Bathe a mild sunburn in vinegar, or give your child a tepid bath.
- Apply aloe vera to the affected area.
- Dress your child in loosely fitting clothes.
- Give your child baby aspirin if the pain persists.

Teething
- Give your child a teether to chew on. Here are some suggestions: hard breadsticks, bagels, biscuits, hard rubber "puppy rings," frozen bananas, and Popsicles.

Temperatures
A normal temperature is 99.6 degrees (rectal reading), 98.6 degrees (oral reading), and 97.6 degrees (underarm reading).
Do the following if your child's temperature is high:
- Bathe your child in tepid (not cold) water. This can be done by immersing your child in the tub or sponge-bathing him/her with a cool washcloth.
- Remove heavy clothes or blankets.
- Give your child baby aspirin (or an aspirin substitute).
- Call your physician if the high temperature persists.

The Umbilical Cord
- Keep diapers below the umbilical cord so the cord will neither be rubbed nor get wet.
- Sponge-bathe your baby until the umbilical cord falls off.

ADMINISTERING AID
Have a doll on hand when you change a bandage or treat an injury.
Encourage your child to give the doll the same treatment he/she is receiving.
This will occupy your child and make it easier for you to administer aid.

Medicines
- Do not take medicine in front of your child. This is so his/her normal response of imitating you will not result in taking medicine without supervision.

- Do not tell your child that medicine is candy or that it is fun to take. This is so he/she will not want to take medicine when it is not necessary.
- Use a hollow, graduated medicine spoon, eyedropper, or syringe to give your infant liquid medicine. Squirt the medicine into the side of the mouth, then gently hold the mouth closed.
- Hold a paper cup under your child's chin when you are giving liquid medicine. The cup will catch any spills. Then you can note how much is in the cup and remeasure the exact amount to add for the full dosage.
- Encourage your child to take pills by crushing them and adding them to honey, jam, or fruit juice.
- Make pills easier to swallow by coating them with butter.

Adhesive Bandages
- Be generous in your use of adhesive bandages as they have a positive psychological effect on children.
- Remove adhesive bandages as soon as possible as fresh air promotes healing.
- Remove adhesive bandages easily after your child's bath, or
- Rub baby oil on the adhesive bandage for easy removal.

Cold Compress
- Freeze wet washclothes in sealable plastic bags and use them for cold compresses.
- Put uncooked rice in a sealable plastic bag, freeze it, and use it as a cold compress.
- Use an unopened can of frozen fruit juice concentrate as a cold compress.

Other Aids
- Have your child use paper plates, cups, straws, and napkins when he/she is ill. These disposables will keep the spread of germs to a minimum.
- Keep a plastic dishpan or wastebasket near your child if he/she might vomit. Place a towel or dropcloth under the container.
- Feel free to spend the night in your child's room if he/she is ill. Your presence may be a comfort and help to you both.

THE DOCTORS

Be prepared to give this information to the doctor when you call. Tell him/her your
- name
- child's name
- child's age
- child's present temperature
- child's present symptoms (include physical appearance, mood, sleep pattern, and eating pattern)
- pharmacist's name and telephone number

HOSPITALS

- Arrange a field trip with your child to the hospital. Visit the emergency room, have lunch in the cafeteria, and possibly buy him/her something from the hospital gift shop. Hopefully, this pleasant experience will give your child a positive attitude toward hospitals and will make him/her more receptive and cooperative during hospitalization or emergency treatment.
- Remember that parents have a legal right to stay nights as well as days with their hospitalized children. If you choose to do this, you may want to share the responsibility with your spouse.
- Help your hospitalized child feel comfortable and secure by allowing him/her to bring favorite things from home (for example, a toy, a doll, a blanket, a pillow).
- Stack wrapped surprises on your child's bedside table. Let your child open one package on each day of his/her hospital stay. Try to include items and activities that are suitable to use in the hospital.
- Let friends and relatives know exactly when and where your child is in the hospital. Encourage them to write or visit your child.